SCARING UP THE MORNING

Poems

Scaring up the Morning

Poems

Bruce McEver

LIBRARY OF CONGRESS CATALOGUING
IN PUBLICATION DATA
Scaring Up the Morning/McEver, Bruce
Poetry. Poems.
ISBN 10: 1-936196-22-0
ISBN 13: 978-1-936196-22-7
LCCN: 2001012345

C&R Press
812 Westwood Ave.
Suite D
Chattanooga, TN 37405
www.crpress.org

Book Design: Travis Denton
Cover art: *Impression Sunrise*, 1872, Claude Monet

In partnership with Eco-Libris, 100 trees
have been planted toward the creation of
this book. For more about Eco-Libris and
making reading more sustainable, please
visit www.ecolibris.net.

A Note of Gratitude:

The shape of these poems comes from a circle of poets around my good friend, Thomas Lux, who I met over a decade ago at a workshop at the *92nd Street Y* in New York. There are a number of poets, all friends of Tom's, who teach at the Sarah Lawrence Summer Writer's Workshop, who helped bring some of these poems to maturity, notably Chard deNiord, a fellow divinity school grad who has kindly written the introduction for this book, but also Stephen Dobyns, Stuart Dischell and Kevin Pilkington. And special thanks to Kurt Brown who helped me write and assemble the chapbook, *Quartet for Daniel*, which appears in this book.

Tom's associate, the former drummer, Associate Director of Poetry @ TECH, Travis Denton, has helped me edit this work and has additionally designed the book, its layout, and cover. Travis was indispensable in the production of this work and connected me with Chad Prevost, who along with his partner Ryan Van Cleave at C&R Press, chose to publish and promote the book. I offer my special thanks to Ryan and Chad—their keen eyes and editorial comments are much appreciated.

For my mother Lucille

Contents

III.

IV.

FORWARD

With a quiet yet resonant voice and keen eye, Bruce McEver takes careful notice of his subjects, which range from flowers to Buddhist temples, tea rooms to beggars, apple trees to skinny dipping. Yet, behind this tangible subject matter—what William Carlos Williams referred to metaphorically as the "twiggy stuff of bushes"—lie affections that McEver wisely chooses to evoke through vivid lyrical description, loaded imagery, and studied observation over mere telling and embellished declaration. In his poem titled "Winter Orchard," a spare primer that strikes the middle C of his patient self-assaying, McEver sums up the grievous yet hopeful conceit of *Scaring Up the Morning*.

> Dormant trees survive winter's clutch,
> their burgeoning red-budded branches
> arched high and partly pruned
> made ready for spring.
> Like a father's approval withheld
> from an eager boy,
>   or a wife lost,
> he's been hard trimmed.
>
> Raw juice, so gusty,
> a glass a day cleanses through stinginess,
> prepares me for the thaw
> to savor earth's sweet gifts
> and imagine
>   the blossoming.

In the four sections that comprise *Scaring Up the Morning*, McEver moves thematically from pastoral and familial meditations in the first section to military, religious, political, and geological topics in section two—topics that follow a similar meditative thread in their various lyrical analyses, to a four part threnody in section three for a boy named Daniel afflicted with Rhabdomyoscaroma, to love poems for his new wife in section four. Throughout these sundry sections, McEver maintains a consistently steady gaze from his compassionate lookout, approaching his grief, his past, his faith, his job as a continent hopping business man, his joy with a deliberate, but engaging perspicacity like a most generous tour guide through both his gardens and "desert places." Whether at the market in Ubud, Bali

> …that smells of incense and spices,
> and jumbled with women selling saffron sarongs
> and scarves, to buy a canang,
> a small palm-leaf tray
> of offering flowers.

or pausing before a stripped car that is

> a memorial of early loves
> transformed into a large flower pot
> for sprays of oleanders and hibiscus
> triumphant,
> now pecked over by a cock
> and some scrawny chickens

McEver writes generously and with very little "irritable reaching," divining a language of acceptance over contention, plain witnessing over embellishment, with a hard won equipoise. These poems betray admirable preparation for the poetic task at hand, namely, the patient, courageous attention and emotional girding necessary for viewing both the ordinary and unknown with the requisite "cold eye" the muse demands. McEver knows this implicitly, but describes it for his reader and himself as a kind of credo that is less self-consciously poetic than philosophically, even religiously true. "I soon come into silence," he writes in the concluding stanza of "Year of the Rooster,"

> And find a presence all around,
> in each empty stone seat,
> high on the pagoda platforms,
> silhouetted by the far volcano,
> that invites the mystery—
> no—becomes the mystery
> those roosters scare up
> each morning.

—Chard deNiord
November, 2012

WINTER ORCHARD

The scent of just juiced apples
rationed during a fast, joins
me with an orchard frozen at attention
outside my window in a March snow.
Dormant trees survive winter's clutch,
their burgeoning red-budded branches
arched high and partly pruned,
made ready for spring.
Like a father's approval withheld
from an eager boy,
                          or a wife lost,
he's been hard trimmed.

Raw juice, so gusty,
a glass a day cleanses through stinginess,
prepares me for the thaw
to savor earth's sweet gifts
and imagine
              the blossoming.

I

YEAR OF THE ROOSTER

I

In Bali, a chorus of roosters conspire
to raise the sun and divine
each morning of the world.
A golden hue lumens the palm tangle
edging terraced rice patties,
stacked like pancakes and soggy
from an irrigation system
shared since antiquity.

I visit the Ubud market,
that smells of incense and spices,
and jumbled with women selling saffron sarongs
and scarves, to buy a canang,
a small palm-leaf tray
of offering flowers.

I make a path through the hawkers
of batik and sandalwood carvers
to a forest at the end of town.
Drawn by the sound of water spewing
from a crevice in the ground
I wander down mossy stairs.

Over the cascade, arches a bridge
whose rails are stone serpents.
They crawl through a square portal
cut in the airy root veil
of a banyan tree spanning
the holy stream.

Beyond this portal, stands a stone sanctuary
where I bathe with other worshippers

in a clear pool fountain-headed by marbled dragons
to wash away my travel husk
and demons and pray.

I dry and wrap the requisite sarong
and tie a sash around me to cross
the temple threshold opening us
to the sky like a plea.
Barefoot, I enter the inner temple yard
scattered with alters wrapped
in black-checked and bright-yellow cloths.

II

The priest, white turbaned
and robed, rings a bell
to punctuate incantations.
I sit cross-legged to address the presence
in the prescribed manner.
I cleanse my hands in the smoking ember
of my incense stick next to my canang
and clasp the proper flower
to my forehead before tossing it away.

White first, for the Great One,
then amber and mauve
for lesser and local gods.
I am careful not to offend anyone,
under the gaze of fierce
stone temple guardians.
Irreverent monkeys play
over the inner sanctum.

I soon come into the silence
and find a presence all around,
in each empty stone seat,
high on the pagoda platforms,
silhouetted by the far volcano,
that invites the mystery—
no—becomes the mystery
those roosters scare up
each morning.

SUNFLOWERS

The sun god's seedy-eyed children
strain at their stalks
daily to follow the light,
east to west, in unison.
Late summer days, their great heads droop,
tired and weighty.

In neat rows behind the house
with peeling blue paint,
their yellow bonnets exude cheer.
They seem out of place
in an unkempt yard of scattered toys and car parts
crowned by a Chevy carcass with spoiler.

There's a tractor and snow plough
for sale, down at the street,
next to the family's
honor vegetable stand,
where they sell those sunbursts:
the gay heads they chop off
to make ends meet.

MANY PATHS

...that very Spirit intercedes
with sighs too deep for words.
　　　　—Romans 8:26

Christmas morning, below zero,
the day after she died,
my breath freezing, I am dazed
as I walk into the barnyard,
to recall our happiness with the animals there.
Sagging cedar gates close behind me.

My quarter horse, Cinnamon,
spots me over a hundred yards distant
and begins his long lope. Soon,
his soft nuzzle is rubbing my face, warm,
then her horse and soon, the whole herd,
joined by the goats, and the dog.
They ring me in a circle of compassion.

Touched, yet unbelieving, I look up
into a blinding, cold sun and feel a release—
an energy courses
the length of my body,
and something says again, then again:
There are many paths.

Nothing has ever been so clear.

DELRAY BEACH

Where pelicans patrol the space over sand and sea,
gliding in prehistoric formation,
like old PBYs my uncle flew in WWII.
Sharp-eyed, they peel off
and plunge into the waves.

I bike along the inter-coastal waterway
where yachts at anchor seem posed
for mutual fund ads. Both sides
of the road are chock-a-block with condos
leaving little of the native mango hammock
between this path and the water save
some landscaped
sea grapes and gumbo-limbos.

High rises top the dunes down the coast,
like Manhattan moved south.
And above block-like towers, buzzards
feather afternoon thermals,
unemployed and patient for road kill.

Up from their naps, the snow birds
walk the beach afternoons,
their tracks soon smoothed by the surf.
Retired from work and winters,
their time's suspended, slowed
like the traffic waiting for those yachts
to parade under yawning drawbridges.

Along this path, trees are cenotaphs to departed
snowbirds with their dates on a plastic plaque.
I want to know their stories though:
that third date,
when they gave up the hassle
and came down here for good,
content to walk
           by the sea.

HARLEM VALLEY

An abandoned mental hospital rises
from wetlands invaded by a canebrake.
A town of ramshackle houses and trailers, grown up
like untrimmed hedges around the red-brick dorm shells.
Each time the train stops here
I recall a friend whose mother survived it.

The criminally insane are still holed up
behind razor-wire wrapping the big house on the hill.
Once dedicated by the governor, the proud power plant
stack stands a phallic, smokeless sentry,
graffitied, across the tracks.

Seeking budget cuts, politicians
set the non-violent inmates free.
Today in the city, those not taken in
by their families, mumble discontent, digging
through garbage cans, homeless
and missing their predictable wards.

Retread as auto mechanics and deli waitresses,
their former wardens miss them too.
They remember nirvana nights
when "No Vacancy" on the marquee
of the Starlight Inn meant a full tavern.

My friend missed her teenage years.
Obliged to raise seven siblings,
she'd visit her mom, hoping for progress:
Mother, tell me this won't happen to me.

But she was drugged,
and after shock treatments,
could only stare
and manage a smile.

AT THE BOHEMIAN GROVE

members boast the redwood root mass
mothering this grove's over ten thousand years old.
It's the Methuselah remnant of a primeval
forest that once reached the Rockies,
progenitor of the Petrified Forest.

Redwoods are impervious to fire, invasive,
and fierce competitors. In a dryer age,
they retreated to the California coast
where they could live off the fog.

Settlers clear-cut surrounding stands
to build San Francisco. The new city's elite
Bohemian Club members traveled
to this grove on empty returning lumber cars.

Old photos show them, mostly mustached,
spilling off the rail platform to picnic, play
and hike among great stumps. For nearly a century,
Bohemians witnessed the re-growth
of this great tree cathedral.

Today, legacies in a hundred tented camps
gather as summer bachelors around their great owl mascot
hearing words of wisdom and wit from the distinguished.
Multi-talented, they act, perform symphonies, and sing.

Afterwards, they dine in luminous
gas-lit circles, between huge pillars of trees
at tables of fine fellowship,
imbibing California's best wines,

pausing when nature calls to water
their ancient brothers with impunity.

THE STRESS REDUCTION CENTER

I creak up the stairs
of a white frame walk-up on Clement.
In a side-split gown, the hostess
oversees a desk with a plastic waterfall.
I pay up front and she ushers me
into a room with a sheet-draped table
and face cradle and insists I disrobe.

Jasmine enters and in halting English
introduces herself. With talented toes,
she dances down my spine,
holding onto a jungle gym
bolted to the ceiling. She tramps
out my vintage sorrow,
while in the background—
the words of the prophets
are written on the subway walls.

Thirty years ago, that same song blared,
driving my bride across the Bay Bridge
to our first home, a Navy duplex
on Yerba Buena Island.
There, under fragrant eucalyptus,
in our backyard we ate local crab
off newspapers watching
the container ships maneuver to port.

Like the China Hauler I watched
last evening bisect the orange spans
of the Golden Gate and fade
into the Pacific fog bank,
so I watched my wife fade
                into unconsciousness.

ALONG THE SALMON KILL

Be doers of the word, and not merely hearers
who deceive themselves.
—James 1:22

Autumn Sunday, alone, biking in praise
of the golden mantle draping
this valley, cut and coursed
by the dark stream running
through my adopted town,
its pure waters offered in a white
marble drinking fountain next to town hall.

The kill borders the Scoville library
the oldest public library in the country
and whose chimes honor my late wife.
Across the street, the Puritan church
that founded and centered Salisbury in 1744
where this morning the sermon exampled
James's letter extolling action.

I think of the impossibility
of language capturing the color
and flare of the maples in this valley,
lined up like gaudy guard soldiers
for sugar bushes. Farms
still demarcated by stonewalls
keeping cattle wandering green pastures,
dumbfounded by a cyclist, and slobbering
from drinking the same cold waters.
It hastens on by tumbled furnace ruins,
once stoked steel melt hot
by bellows turned by the branch,
spilling into a silver sheet
over a colonial constructed dam.

These townsfolk feared God,
but not foreign overlords
who forbade their steel making.
They poured cannon, then rails that took their works
east to Hartford and on west to war.
Doers, not hearers leave stone walls.

II

MONARCH MIGRATION

It seemed a miracle, a sign,
a butterfly fluttering out the window,
behind Yevtushenko reading poems,
then confessing his secret: his best works
are motivated by shame and love.

Back in my office, more Monarchs flutter
south through Manhattan's towered forest.
In Central Park, orange bunches
refuel on purple asters
sensing they must move on before frost.

Each year, ahead of thermal gradients,
some decipherer of longitude, implanted
in their ganglia, guides orange throngs
to fir stands in Mexico's mountains.

If these flutterers get there,
they breed and die in trees.
In spring, their offspring fly back
through the south, hunting milkweed
for laying eggs. A third generation
breaks pods and takes off
for long-day Canadian summers
where the cycle repeats.

Their risks escalate.
Storms blow them off course;
herbicides deplete the milkweed;
and the firs are lumbered.

Despite all, Monarchs pass on
their secret of navigating the length
of the Americas over generations,
fulfilling the ancient Aztec prophecy:
warriors who die in battle,
return from heaven
as butterflies.

BUSINESS CLASS

Like a flying morgue,
we lie blanketed
in leathered recliners,
5x5, L.A. to Sidney.
In the indigo glow
of our in-flight monitors,
we sleep exhausted, flipped
through all multi-lingual channels.

Please, no more hot, roasted nuts,
smoked salmon or chef-endorsed
entrées with wine pairings.
The port, aged cheese
and duty-free did us in.

Our bodies snug with booties
issued from our ditty kits,
we hurtle supine across the Pacific,
unconsciously crossing
the Date Line, losing
a day of our lives.

Perhaps it fell into some volcanic fold
between atolls and tectonic plates,
into a deep sea crevasse in the Coral Sea?

And what of our final journey,
when we pass through the glass darkly,
losing all time?
Can we honestly fill out
that customs form declaring
our hearts weigh
less than a feather?

THE QUEEN'S REUNION

Sidney *rocks* slide down nice with local brew.
Across the bay from a steel backdrop
of red, black, and white liner, we dine
at the Oyster bar on Circular Quay.
The whole city celebrates the reunion
of two great queens who met up
in this harbor last during the second world war
to ferry Aussie troops to battle.

These floating palaces
travel oceans like elegant ideas.
Mary arrived at sunrise, Elizabeth at sunset,
escorted by a sprawl of boats and yachts,
and a swarm of helicopters.
A red fireboat drum majored the procession
arching spray in three directions.

Dapper, handsome dressed in Harris tweed,
with tan polished shoes, and sporting a bowtie,
the old man sits on a quay bench through the hubbub.
His buddy leans on a cane;
they seem a pair from the Veterans' home.

He's annoyed by Japanese girls sharing his bench.
The girls photograph themselves and capture him
as well, showing him their photos. They giggle
their odd way, cupping hands over mouths.
He pretends not to notice.

Perhaps he remembers that day in 1939
when the great ships were here before.
With backpack and rifle slung over his shoulder,
he left for Burma kissing goodbye
the girl, he would never see again.

He survived hell
building that damned bridge
over the Kwai for the Japanese
after his capture.

That's why he's here today:
quietly sunning his Australian spirit,
big as any big boat,
big as the outback.

ON FOX GLACIER

I squint at the icy spines
of the Fox Glacier shimming white
up its back to the New Zealand mountain top.
Like a frozen dragon regurgitated
from the lowest rungs of Dante's hell,
this holdover from the ice age,
defends its turf against global warming.

Chill breaths down the entire valley it sculpts,
even browns tree ferns in the rain forest below.
The size of the cavernous cerulean
mouth and crevasses awe.
A little gray and dirty around the edges,
it devours boulders and reduces
them to gravel, grist
for the milky lapidary melt
spilling down the excavation.

This river of ice, the pack
of thousands of years of snow,
advances winters, and retreats
summers in a geological rhythm
confounding conventional time.

Wearing down defiant granite,
it grinds to smooth submission
mountain and valley alike,
determined like its ancestors who polished up
Central Park and Yosemite, all these
vassals from the kingdom of cold.

THE RETURN OF THE SAMURAI

Having sealed his deal,
the samurai sprawls
on the yellow chaise by the aqua pool
at the Raffles Hotel. The towers
of Singapore stand at attention
ringing its bay that holds squadrons
of freighters and tankers,
nursed by sampans.

Tourists crowd a river statue
on the quay below,
where the mythic Merliton spews a salute,
a half lion/half sea beast
that challenged the city's legendary founder.

Nearby, a memorial for citizens
executed by the Japanese;
but no memorial stands
for the Japanese bicycle battalions who peddled
through steaming jungles to surprise
the British defenders with their guns
facing out to sea.

The samurai businessman relaxes
into the sounds of his iPod,
takes a slow drag from his Lark
and scatters squeamish Americans
and fussy Brits with a cloud.

A dark waiter with neat white turban
marches a Bloody Mary
to his low teak table and bows,
happy to be of service.

BEGGAR MAN

Hong Kong is a spew
of silver and glass towers,
stainless steel posts that overpopulate
the mountain sides rimming its harbor.
Bound together by concrete ribbons of roads and ramps,
The city's kinetic with crowds, double-decker buses,
rickshaws and red-checkered cabs
whose back doors pop open to salute you.

Stacked-high container ships,
tended by lighters and tugs, play
dodge with junks and the Star Ferry
in the blue-green bay
being filled in for yet more buildings.

Pedestrian ramps and bridges,
are scurries of shoppers
between malls and towers.
A twisted beggar manages
to climb onto a walkway at rush hour
and blows on his little plastic pipe.

He plays no particular tune.
A worn hat seeded with a few coins,
and his contorted body
keep him from being trampled.
Weary, he crawls back
to his corner of blankets and rags,
next to a steaming noodle shop
behind all this glitter and go.

BEFORE THE BEES SWARM

At the Shuanglin Temple bees
laze beneath the round roof
tiles, arched like bamboo wings, smoked
with incense from a bronze pot.
They are at peace with tourists, who wander
the courtyard, snapping photos
and admiring the auras
of a chorus of bodhisattvas—
a thousand Buddha's who gaze
through time's slow dust.

Each porcelain's a personality,
because their monk-makers
wanted to show all can be
enlightened harmoniously
through self knowledge. Unlike
the hordes carrying little red books—
those who would erase this history
and build a new collective future—
those who attacked,
but spared this temple.

If anyone renovates this place
and cleans the coal dust from these statues,
their original colors would vanish
and the bees swarm.
With the striking of the prayer gong,
the Buddhas' stare through me.

Leaving, our bus bounces along
a tollway, staged with double rows
of poplar and pine.
It is packed with convoys
of tarped red trucks, heavy

with the coal of Shanxi.
Traveling along the Yellow river,
sunflowers are planted in rows
between cornfields like humble
Chinese serving girls,
drooping their heavy heads.
A few stand tall and golden,
communing directly with the sun,
through the haze, trying
to be flowers, not fodder.

And as we cross the river over
a lyre-like bridge,
a new city of high rises
emerges and marches through
the coal haze, across the plain

like the emperor's army.
Impressive, row upon row,
block after block, as far
as the eye sees

grey and brown pylons
of honey-combed humanity.
Under construction:
homes of harmony—
the fruit of the last five year plan,
the Red Dream rising.

THE PEOPLE'S PARK

Off Nanking Road, the divide
between the French and British concessions
in Shanghai, western ads abound:
L'Octaine and Barberry, BNP and HSBC still
compete for storefronts, billboards and billionaires.
Chinese characters, no longer chic—
banished from the road,
beyond the People's Park,
where I walk at first light.

The park is full of choreographed Tai Chi troops,
stepping and spinning through their dream-like routines:
"wave hands like cloud" or "repulse monkey."
A sculptured rock garden with a tea house
on a gold-and-orange-carp-schooled pond
has the slow dancers all over its paths,
behind the plantings, as human leaves
imitating wind, gracefully concentrating,
seeking to be one with the flow,

to touch the force
that inspires bird song and vanishes
with the morning smog,
that balances opposites
on the cusp of the yin and yang
the Tao, the Way,
before brands became gods.

HOLIDAY PARTY

Go-go dancers in Santa bikinis grind
around chromed poles stationed
about the mansion's grounds.
Above the crush of crowd,
they bend and blend with the hubbub
at my old classmate's Palm Beach bash.

A little stoned, he can't remember me at first,
but soon recalls arranging our class trips,
seeing us off before dawn, earning his way
through Harvard the hard way.
Tonight, he's arrived and adopted
the town to celebrate his new blonde friend,
who welcomes us to her palazzo by the sea.

Overwhelmed with traffic, police send valets
scampering to empty the line-up of Rolls and Jags
spilling legions of open-shirted
and sequined guests.
They filter through tables of welcoming booze
and squadrons of servants with canapés on silver trays.

The cigar clique puffs disbelief in the billiard parlor,
What does this guy do?
Their well-cleavaged and bejeweled ladies dip
strawberries into a chocolate fountain.
They grin with surgically sculpted smiles,
breathless.

It is still early in the evening
when the party spills serpentine
onto the beach in a barefoot conga line,
crooning with the band
to a big moonrise.

WAR GAMES

*"Israel carried out a major military exercise
earlier this month that officials say appeared
to be a rehearsal for a potential bombing
attack on Iran's nuclear facilities."*
—*The New York Times*
June 20, 2008

When our fleet divided for nuclear exercises,
I was focsle watch aboard the missile frigate Kerry.
We sailed for the opposite ends of the Med to search out
and annihilate one another.

We spearheaded the Blue Navy, sailing near Point Sunion,
beneath its Poseidon temple ruins,
where for millennia, Greeks, then Romans
incensed and petitioned victory prayers.
I feel the seaweed festooned god,
astride the prow of our sleek warship, steaming
full ahead to battle alongside ancient brothers.

I imagine I'm a citizen oarsman on an Athenian trireme
staying the Persian onslaught; I'm with Ptolemy
in the mayhem at Action;
or I'm on forecastle with Nelson,
about to cross the "T" at Trafalgar.

But then, a dot on the horizon.
In my binoculars, an F-4 screams into focus,
supersonic, straight for us, topping the swells,
rendering our radar impotent.

Before I can shout: *Bogie at 12 o'clock!*
he nails us, kicks in his after-burners,
goes vertical in a roar.
Less than an hour after the war began,

the game was over.
We were nuked,
our pretension vaporized
to a soft sea breeze.

SPACE SHOT

There, across the darkness
of Florida's palmetto scrub,
poised to launch, the Discovery
stars in the bright Zeon floodlights.
It nurses an orange tank
of frothing gases twice its size.
Its boosters, like giant Roman candles,
stand at the ready to escort
the shuttle into orbit.

Jets roar through the cloud cover
to vouchsafe a stubborn ceiling.
Nervously, throngs watch
from the beaches and stands for the blast
that will turn night into day.

Was this excitement in the crowds
at Verona harbor in 1492,
waiting for three small ships
to catch favorable winds
and disappear over horizon?

Our spotlighted technology-idol
smokes eerily and silent.
Aboard, seven bright-suited astronauts
are strapped in and eager to re-man
an international space station.
As the window of opportunity
narrows, no prayers are said,
no censors swung.

Technicians and scientist ritually
check two million systems that must sync
during the ten hour countdown they control:

A-OK in Houston, down range CLEAR,
and in the consoled firing room at the Cape,
screens glow green, a GO,
but the clouds have their arms crossed.
The window's passed:
                    Stand down.

SOUL WRESTLER

The moat, mounds, palisade and balustrade
are still visible under the matrix of moss-hung oaks,
shading the tabby-shell ruins of the fortress town.

It was in these "undecided lands"
between the superpowers of that age
where the British backed Oglethorpe's utopian
experiment, the colony of Georgia.
Here, they stamped a 40-acre star-shaped fortress,
like a Christmas cookie cut from the marshes
at Sea Island on the banks of the Frederica
to wrestle this land from the Indians and Spain
as they did at Bloody Marsh.

Journals say John Wesley
was called with his brother, Charles,
to be Oglethorpe's chaplains.
On their crossing, they were impressed by the faith
of Moravians' facing a storm.
John's first sermon here
was preached on this subject
under an oak outside town.

There were few congregants that first day,
but by the next Sunday, the crowd spilled
from the shadow of the great tree.
John believed faith transformed all
rich, poor, slave, or Indian—Jesus, after all,
shared his bread and wine.

A failed love affair sent John back to England.
But the fire of his new faith, kindled in Georgia,
he spread to the throngs left
in industrialism's wake.

He preached outside factories,
to whomever would listen, igniting
a new evangelic movement, the "Methodist."

Like disciples, Wesley's word spread
by his itinerant circuit riders, circled the globe,
and back to Georgia. John Wesley,
the man who wrestled for souls
in the shade of these oaks.

THE BARD

takes inspiration from the newly-greened
canopy of elms dappling his statue in Central Park.
The endangered forest, like a troop
of dervishes is frozen in their devotion,
with arms whirling akimbo and palms up in praise.
Unfazed, Robbie, seeking the right turns of phrase,
sits on a bronze stump, next to his plow
(the one that had a run-in with the mouse)
in knee socks and brogans, penning
illicit lines to Mary with a quill.

Born a dirt farmer in Ayshire,
he captured the brogue and the unflagging
spirit of the Scotts, then thinned
by the Clearances, like the elms from their blight.
And he, always aflame for a fair lassie,
passionate till his early demise,
of consumption, was inspired
to pearls of poetry. Like an oyster,
he refined from the grist of poverty,
the highland ballads and songs,
into *Auld Lang Syne* and elegant toast
in the service of haggis.

PRAYER FLAGS

Lhasa, Tibet
July, 2004

Just landed and leadened with oxygen sickness,
I climb its Acropolis, to the Portola,
the Dalai Lama's winter palace.
It is painful to breathe, to put one foot forward,
but imagining thousands of saffron robed monks
once chanting up there keeps me going.

In an inner chamber, a painting
depicts the Tibetan peoples' origins from monkeys.
A playful and prayerful lot,
they decorate their land above the tree line
with prayer flags of symbolic colors.

Up the shoulders of ridge trails, at every turn,
cairns hold these tattered scraps,
colorful sacred scarecrows.
Flags fly from poles on corners of Tibetan homes
with smoke curling from central hearths, a prayer to heaven.
Tattered bits of cloth, blue for sky, red, earth,
green for water, and yellow, spirit, pray.
Farmyards with adobe walls hold the family fortune:
scrawny chickens, a withered cow, shaggy yak.

Their windows wear heavy eyeliner,
like the all-seeing eye of Buddha.
Monks spin prayer wheels for tourists and wink,
sneaking us little gold framed glimpses
of His Holiness under the folds of their robes.

But on the way to the airport, our bus
falls behind a military convoy;

red-starred liberators on maneuvers
allow no one to break their ranks.
Scraps of cloth on hillsides
flap in a stiff breeze,
praying they will someday
find their way home.

TEMPLE TURTLE

Between appointments,
I chance upon a shrine
near the Tokyo Stock Exchange.
Perhaps a firestorm survivor,
cramped between modernity's jumble
of stores and offices,
like an old fence grown into a tree.
Its ancient roof tiles tilt toward heaven
confused by a scramble
of raised highways and telephone lines.

Centered, before the sanctuary,
large cow-like bells, tasseled
to thick ropes, summon
the residing Kami
to grant a good examination,
a job promotion or even save
a short-squeezed broker.

A large donation box stands
ready to receive the beneficence.
The reverent come, bow, ring the bells,
step back, bow again, and clap
to be sure fortune falls their way.

Leaving, a couple takes water
in a bamboo ladle
from a burbling spring
near the entrance gate,
and notice a tortoise,
his shell echoing the ancient roof tiles,
looking up through ageless eyes,
humbled the world's
been taken off his back.

III

QUARTET FOR DANIEL

I. Miracle at the Canaan VFW

The white battle star
on the turret of the Sherman tank parked
outside the VFW is a beacon
through this sleety evening for the citizens of Canaan
lining up for a $5-a-plate spaghetti dinner.

The townsfolk turned out after work
from factories, farms and shops,
in overalls, flannel shirts and calico frocks.
They come so my farmer-neighbor's boy, Daniel,
age 13, might survive the cancer
his surgeon couldn't cut out.

The spit-polished Marine auxiliary
regulate seating and raffle chances
on donations from maple syrup to lawn services,
all tracked on a board like the Stock Exchange.
The church's upkeep society sells
home-baked cookies and cakes.
Boy scouts and girl scouts serve
heaped plates of noodles globed
with sweet plum tomato sauce.

While his separated parents fight
over custody, the townspeople adopt the boy,
ready to fight his battle—
Rhabdomyoscaroma.

And like the defenders
of Thermopylae or the Alamo,
surrender's no option.

II. The Christening

Behind three red gothic doors,
Daniel's family and friends gather
around the baptismal font
as the priest in starched linen sprinkles
holy water from the marble basin
on Daniel's new half-sister, Holly.
She burbles, unaware of her role
as angel of hope.
Her three half-brothers look on,
squirming in ill-fitting blazers
and unaccustomed ties.

As we drive to the reception together,
Daniel tells me he's in remission
so we talk future plans: *I wish*
I didn't have to wait until I was 15 ½
to get my driver's license, he complains.
What do you want to do with it anyway?

Well, to start a landscaping service in the spring.

What do you want to be when you grow up?
I probe further and he looks at me straight:

A Senator.

III. The Phaedo

Daniel picks me up
in his father's chassis-stripped
truck with the Confederate flag.
His face is puffy and contorted
from the recurrent tumor. He speaks
from the side of his mouth.
A blue plaid hunters hat, flaps askew,
covers his chemo-bald head.

We bounce back up the rutted road
to their log cabin, still hung
in last year's Christmas lights.
He bounds the stairs past
Holly's stroller and his wheelchair
with the IV bag hanger for hospital trips.

We sit in the living room littered
in baby toys from the play pen.
I decided not to take any more chemo.
I need a life and that stuff makes me bad sick.
I'm not afraid because I have the medallion
you gave me that Mother Teresa blessed.
I pray to God and Jesus every night
and don't think they will let anything bad happen.
Some day they will come for my soul, anyway.

I probe young Socrates for his views
of afterlife relating a dream
I had shortly after my wife passed:
she returned escorted by three bear guardians
and told me she had another job
now protecting the animals.

I have a mission too,
Daniel says unhesitatingly,
I'm going to come back and protect
the farmers and their crops.
That's what I'm called to do.

IV. Preparing for the Next Life

I'm surprised when Daniel's mom phones,
eager for me to take him to the tractor store.
The tumor has grown and with talking now painful,
he has to write down words.

At the cabin, he greets me
with his jacket on and slurring, *there's not much time.*
He wants to be sure everything's in stock
for his landscaping business come spring.

When we arrive, Daniel climbs
onto one of fifty tractors after surveying the lot.
The manager muses: *He's picked the exact*
one I'd recommend for this job,
and extols its virtues as Daniel motions for paper
to list the accessories he needs.

Daniel's on a mission, yanking equipment
off the racks, stacking
a roto-tiller, chain saw, weed whacker,
and leaf blower outside the manager's office.

Sitting together in front of the manager's desk,
I'm not sure why I'm there
and Daniel, with his contorted face
looks like the Elephant Man,
yet calm and business-like, reviewing
the tally, his blue-plaid hunters cap askew.

Being November, we take the blower,
but Daniel's now too weak to give it a crank.
I take him home, and he barely manages the stairs.
The nurse asks where we've been.
He grins, gives me a handshake and a hug.

The next night, he is gone.

RETURN TO CANAAN

The tractor store's lot is moguled
under snow. The marquis
of the town's cinema announces
it's reopening as a dinner theater.
And in daylight, the VFW's trophy,
battle tank seems an oversized toy.

Over the stubbly cornfield
across from Daniel's house, a hawk gyres.
His father and grandfather butcher a fatted calf,
with a chain, hung, headless
from the lip of their tractor-loader.
The red-marbled carcass swings and steams,
shrouded in a mist rising
off thawing fields
as winter beats
an early retreat.

IV

THE TAO

The amber rim of morning
illumines a mist shrouding
the mountain's foot. A will-o'-the-wisp,
as if shy of revelation,
retreats through fall-yellowed woodlands
into the valley of two rivers
bearing mysteries
learned at a master's feet.

Like a recurring dream
searched for meaning,
it steals the ordinary of the day,
robbing routine, insistent
on interpretation.

The shape-shifting cloud,
says: *Slow, consider*
the urgency of those great flocks
veeing South—

what drives
these dawn treaders
disappearing into the mist?

Like an ancient landscape
painted on a parchment scroll,
you recognize the fabled land,
once forgotten,
        the way,
             now before you.

FOUR SKETCHES OF JAPAN

I

The scent of opening apricot,
a bonus of pink sprays,
intoxicate the morning's chill.
We sit on woven mats in a tea house
drinking the warm,
laboriously prepared brew,
our souls steeping
over the temple we just toured.
We are loath to board our bus
in formation with others in the parking lot,
beyond this perfection.

II

Girdled in a woven grass knot
like a sumo wrestler,
it was the centuried cedar,
that impressed us most.
Beneath it a young couple presented
their new baby for blessing
by a white robed priest.
The occasion is made more auspicious
by grandparents photographing every detail.

Here, two religions coexist:
Shinto shrines like this one,
with bright orange gates
called torii
are for life's events.
In the Buddhists' temples,
they bury their dead.

III

We are amazed by the great Buddha's
long earlobes at Nara,
but there's no place to meditate
as the enlightened one advised.
Instead, guides with little flags,
move tourist in brigades
like samurai armies to battle.
Outside sacred deer con us out of biscuits.
Polite girls in kimonos
guess our fortunes and sell us charms
for passing our next exam.

IV

Moss leavened paths to Ryoani temple,
calm by their deep greenness.
Here, unfathomable rocks float
in a raked pebble ocean.
It may represent the universe
or a collusion of creator monks.
Sitting on cedar smoothed
by four centuries of contemplation,
I hold your hand and realize
when the burgeoning cherry bough
hanging over the wall buds,
our worlds will be complete.

CINDERELLA REVISITED

The jeer of a sea gull greets us
as we step off the Jitney into the anonymity
of a cloudy March Saturday.
No one to meet us, but a car's left
to provision ourselves for the weekend.

Shuttered for the season, Hampton's
houses cold-shoulder us.
Shingled with weathered cedar, the mansion line-up
awaits spring's re-opening
behind a filigree of bare-twigged privet.
Pools are canvassed and bushes burlapped from the deer.
A restless sea scrolls empty beaches.

No gargoyles grin when we arrive at your house,
a clean-lined chateau with two chimneys.
No one moves to greet us: your boys absorbed
in a TV hockey game and your sister and her daughter stuck
in a crossword. Your mom's out and will be back late.
Indifference has moved into this house.

Like a servant girl, come to clean
the ashes from these chimneys,
you, quiet and giving, become invisible
working hard, head down, earning
smudged cheeks.

Lucky me, you went out to the ball
that night and sat by me.
You said your slipper was two sizes larger
after birthing two boys—just the size
I was searching for after my first lady passed.
We unwrap our sandwiches
and dine alone, enraptured.

CAR HEAVEN

In Anguilla, a cerulean sea floats
tramp steamers and catamarans.
Palm trees and slow-rusting wrecks
line the port road:
those abandoned autos that escaped
scrap-metal hell and managed
to make it to car heaven.

One green hulk, supine
beside a lime and pink shanty,
looks just like my old car.
A '57 Chevy I souped-up with fuel injection
and added a floor shift and bucket seats.
Freedom with chrome spinners,
it could make home before curfew
on fumes from a quarter's worth of gas.

How did it get here?
Who added a white racing stripe
before stripping it for parts
and turning it over to tether goats?
A memorial of my early loves
transformed into a large flower pot
for sprays of oleanders and hibiscus
triumphant,
now pecked over by a cock
and some scrawny chickens.

FRESH-SQUEEZED ORANGE JUICE

The first morning I spent at my girlfriend's
house in the Hamptons, her mom, Audrey,
made me fresh-squeezed orange juice.
As it was only prepared for her and me,
we bonded over our glasses
and from then on, when I visited
she pulped those half-globes to a healthy glass.

The juicer separated the sweetness
from rind and seed with the stealth
of a grinder. This was a prelude
to our review of the *Times*, swapping sections
at the head of the breakfast table.

When I married her daughter,
that machine was my wakeup call
for catching up on markets and gossip.
One morning in August,

when she could barely make it to the table,
struggling air from one good lung,
but never complaining,
she asked me to make the juice.

With her dulled kitchen knife,
I sectioned the oranges,
ground them on the mandible
with its slipping belt,
and managed two glasses.

The last we sipped together.

IN THE REFLECTING POOL

for Audrey Rosenman
(1934-2007)

Prize water lily hybrids called
Crimson Lady, Pearl Mother, and Goddess of White
bedazzle us, as starburst of color
over the water's still surface.

Beneath them, a school of carp,
radiant orange, like the park's Shinto gate,
feather on gossamer fin.

These brightwater druids
hide under green floating leaves,
and gather around stems from murky depths.
They scatter at our shadows.

As we've scattered from Audrey's
hospital bedside when she fusses and tires
of our confusion and grief.

And like those fish
who know only water,
we cannot see
just above us,
          or behold
               a soul.

SKINNY DIPPING

Yellow flag iris,
wild and invasive fleur-de-lis,
circle my pond. They sun
like a golden crown.

The water's clear and inviting.
The supple trout's glide-paths
lure us down
as they patrol shadows.

Sweating, after a long and humid ride,
it's tempting to strip and revive,
just accept
the discipline of cold.

To renew ourselves
we reveal all:
the naked glory of God's mold,
the winter-appalled flesh,
free from clothes.

We dive through the iris,
the cherubim's fiery swords,
guarding our return
to the time before shame.

WHEN SHE SHOWED ME HER PADDLE

I knew I loved her. The one she earned
at sleep-away camp in Maine, where
her newly remarried parents sent her
to get her out of their hair summers
too early. But she showed them,
winning every honor,
memorialized like merit badges,
little "As" painted on her paddle
for master swimmer, sailor, and canoer.
She climbed every mountain,
walked every path on the camp
and wrote home she was lonely.
One day on a trail, examining
a knotted bundle of pine root, she realized
why they named a little redheaded
Jewish girl, Christina.
That she, indeed like Christ,
has a healing spirit
coursing her veins,
could figure out disease and save people.
And has every day since she was licensed
to wield a scalpel.

SEAGATE

A squadron of pelicans patrol
the slow scroll of swells,
wind surfers, threading
the wave's curling lip, and eyeballing
its water-wall for breakfast.

The ocean's placid horizon
levels all logic, enabling
vast nature to be grasped.
The rain of heaven flows here through a brook.
You lose yourself in its grand design:
that energy, holding it all together,
the compassion lifting the pelican's wing,
the rhythm behind the surf's primordial heartbeat.

You are part of this,
not alone, even close
with this driftwood log where you sit,
betraying its violent past
as a pier, ripped up in a storm,
like your former life,
                              now at rest.

SWEET TEA

for Christina

At harbor side in Port Canaveral,
having waited a week for lift-off,
a free refill's my reward
from the waitress whose tight
NASA tee shirt reads:
Failure is Not an Option.

As I finish my poached eggs,
sleek oversized cruise ships
like beached whales, re-passenger
for the weekly Caribbean run.
They got quite a show last night.

Pelicans riding bobbing boats,
sleep off the excitement
that turned night into day.
The spaceship's shockwave
rousted birds and even caused the fish
to jump in the Banana River.

When the Discovery roared
into the darkness like a star
returning to heaven,
over a million systems had to mesh.

I sip my tea and salute the astronauts
who dock with the space station
this morning, but miss you, my dear,
ours the only system
                    that didn't sync.

THE ORCHID MAN

for S. Robert Weltz
March 6, 1930- March 21, 2010

I

The day before he died,
we walked around your father's
Montecito estate, hoping
the sun and sea breeze would change
the inevitable on the top floor.

From the living room, hushed
in antiques, Chinese screen and red porcelains,
we came into the shade of aged eucalyptus
and passed dormant tennis courts,
scattered with lemons and limes,
as if garden sprites had left in mid-game.

Legend was, the house was shaped like a swastika,
complete with a secret stairway and listening posts,
built by a German flyingace, his three prop totem
steeled on the gates.

Over the manicured lawn, we ambled
and were stunned by a coastal cedar
splintered by the last storm.
Now tangled in its supporting cables, it succumbed,
like a harpooned whale wrapped in draglines.

II

We climbed over its limbs to get to the orchid house,
his reason for moving here, to bring his collection,
outgrowing his Park Avenue apartment,
to the promised land of orchids.

A waft of warm
welcomed us into the anteroom
where his Quotron sat next to watering cans.
Inside, under vaulted glass,
the treasury of rare paphipedilum,
he hybridized of every cross and color
pedestaled on raised beds.
In the slow of ceiling fans,
the field of long-stemmed flowers
swayed, like exotic dancers.

Returning to the house, we climbed
a wide-winding staircase, designed
for the breadth of formal gowns, passing
his partner's desk cluttered
with hand-drawn point and figure charts
and a Bloomberg screen still streaming
red and green with market action.

III

He lay centered on a hospital bed,
slipping in and out of consciousness,
relieved with your presence.
His fourth wife, sat resigned on her bed
in red horn-rims.

Last sunlight filtered by eucalyptus,
illuminated your red hair.
As you stroked his forehead
he apologized for his bad breath,
managed a smile, and asked
his doctor/daughter
for something
to take him
to the other world.

CELEBRATING THE MOON FESTIVAL
AT THE PINGYAO INTERNATIONAL
FINANCIERS' CLUB

Why does the moon tend to be full
when people are apart?
—Su Dong Po, 1076

Over its bar, the Club shows global pretentions:
four clocks tracking time in London,
Moscow, Beijing, and New York,
yet no one speaks Russian anymore,
and barely enough English to manage a red wine.

But here, during the Qing dynasty, the first financiers
gave up their prosperous dye works
after discovering paper
could carry the same value as silver.
They got other merchants to leave deposits
in their vaults who, in turn, traveled
lighter and safer without bodyguards.
Setting out on shaggy horses along ten foot thick walls
that still surround this city,
their clients carryied coded paper
they'd later exchange for coins
at other Rishengchang branches
when they got to Peking,
Nanking, or Chang'an.

And just last night, I strolled those streets
the first bankers left long ago,
past their courtyards of carved screens
and intrigue, protected from plundering Huns
behind the huge walls and watch towers
like an dragon guarding its hoard,
unable to contain an idea that has since
spilled through the earth.

And as predicted, the moon showed up
for her festival, though subdued behind a misty veil.
In honor of the silver goddess
(who carries memories of loved ones)
the city streets were littered with the red rubble
from the autumn festival's fireworks,
bunched and swept away by old women
bent over branch brooms.

This morning, hot water swells green tea leaves
in my cup soon after climbing from a raised bed
to munch a left over moon cake
and I remember her shy appearance
over the curved courtyard eves last night,
inspiring a dream:
a vision stumbling from my bed
this morning and showering first thing,
as my love always does
and did on the other side of the earth
while I watched the shinning.

TULIPS

surprise me like a yellow sunrise,
igniting from my coffee table.
Bought last night in a cold rain,
they stand, radiant, in a tall vase,
leaning toward the window,
savoring the morning light.

How perfectly they spill
with each leaf folded to embrace
the tumbler's edge.
Flown from Holland's fields,
where we biked last spring
between astounding rows of color,

they were the fancy of Turkish sultans.
Gifted to Dutch botanist who
hybridized them to be dazzling:
"tulip mania" became endemic.
Then the deluded traded
their homes for a single bulb.

Today it's big business,
this bounty of bulbs, fresh cut,
and air expressed around the world.
These bright missionaries

come to spread joy
through impersonal cities,
come to roust
from our comfortable beds,
and wake us
from our morning slough.

WHEN THE WOODS WALKED

It was just after dawn illuminated
the yellow-green forest tops unfolding
across from the house on the Little Sandy,
up from the church's immersion pool.
The place is still sweetly haunted
by my late wife and her family,
and surrounded by trees
saved from developers.

It was the sound of the water,
the stream coursing the shoals,
spilling over and smoothing the granite shelf,
that charmed me past mornings
cacophony of birds, excited
by emerging insects.

It was life restarting before me:
the unfolding of little red buds to green
in the tree tops, sponsored by
the vast machinery of trunks,
sucking sap from roots sourced by the stream,
all working right before me.

The trees shared their secret
with me, not their miracle of changing
carbon dioxide to the oxygen,
but they moved first, stepped forward,
reaching through understanding—took me in.

It was as if the ancient Sanskrit texts,
we translated in class, came to life at last.
The wisdom of the Upanishads
poured over me, and I was baptized
on the spot, shouting:

                I am that,

                        I AM THAT!

AUBADE

An orange pearl of light sears
through a morning mist,
ghosting the river.
Its power to renew and refresh,
even forgive yesterday,
glories in the pine-tops.
Earth's diurnal motion lifts
the day's veil.

Unlike most sleep-hung mornings,
something else is here, an awareness,
an arm around your shoulder,
astonishingly there all the time

like the mist streaming up
from the valley, summoned
to higher ground in the pines,
to deliver this message,
and wrap you
unworthy,
               but thankful
                        in its presence.

AUTHOR'S NOTES

Along the Salmon Kill: The distribution of the Dutch-derived term "kill" in New York and New England echoes the colonial settlement of "New Netherland" as well as furnishing half of a specific toponym to the Catskill Mountains. "Scoville" is the family who owned the iron ore mine that sourced the development of the town and region.

Monarch Migration: Monarchs cannot fly below 55°F. Ancient Aztec and Mesoamerican peoples believed the spirits of fallen warriors returned as butterflies and hummingbirds.

Business Class: The ancient Egyptians believed the hearts of departed souls were weighed on a scale against a feather by the gods before being allowed to enter the underworld.

Soul Wrestler: The remains of this tree are now incorporated into a cross at Frederica's Christ Church.

Temple Turtle: A well-known scientist (some say it was Bertrand Russell) once gave a public lecture on astronomy. He described how the earth orbits around the sun and how the sun, in turn, orbits around the center of a vast collection of stars called our galaxy. At the end of the lecture, a little old lady at the back of the room got up and said: "What you have told us is rubbish. The world is really a flat plate supported on the back of a giant tortoise." The scientist gave a superior smile before replying, "What is the tortoise standing on?" "You're very clever, young man, very clever," said the old lady. "But it's turtles all the way down!" Kami: Any of the sacred beings worshiped in Shintoism, conceived as spirits abiding in natural phenomena and sometimes people with extraordinary qualities.

The Bard: Robert Burns (1759-96) was Scotland's national poet and hero. There are more statues of Burns in the USA than any American poet.

Celebrating the Moon Festival: Su Dong Po (Su Shi) is considered to be one of the greatest Chinese poets and probably the foremost all-around genius of the "later" imperial ages. His given name was Su Dong Po and he lived from 1037-1101 during the Song Dynasty. He was a master of prose, poetry, and calligraphy and was a connoisseur of art, cooking, and wines and is considered to be one of the greatest Chinese poets. "Rishengchang" means "Sunrise Prosperity."

When the Woods Walked: The Chandogya Upanishad is one of the "primary" (mukhya) Upanishads of about 200 of these sacred texts of India. Written before 1000 BCE, it contains one of the more important metaphysical messages of the Upanishads, the Mahavakya Tat Tvam Asi ("That art Thou"), establishing the principle of Atman through a dialogue between Uddalaka and his son Shvetaketu. Many metaphors, such as, the illustration of curd and butter, banyan tree and its seed, rivers and ocean, and etc, are given to illustrate the concept of Atman. Within this dialogue, the theory of being (sat) arising from non-being (asat) is refuted and pure, undifferentiated being alone is held as the source of everything. Uddalaka says to his son: "It is from this infinite atom, all that is that Self from end to end. It is the Truth, It is the Self;—Oh, Shevetaketu! THOU ARE THAT."

Acknowledgements:

The author is grateful to the editors of those periodicals in which some of these poems first appeared: "Many Paths" was published by the *Cortland Review*, and "Tulips" appeared in a sermon of mine entitled "Poetry: the Bridge to the Sacred," which appeared in *Parabola Magazine*. "Along the Salmon Kill" appeared in *Meeting House Times* and "In the Reflecting Pool" and "Tulips" were both published by *The Wick* at Harvard. "Year of the Rooster," and "Celebrating the Moon Festival, were published by *Terminus Magazine*.

CPSIA information can be obtained at www.ICGtesting.com
Printed in the USA
LVOW080137220513

334874LV00003B/75/P